Mood Swing, with Pear

Mood Swing, with Pear

SUE MACLEOD

Clarise Foster, Editor

Signature
EDITIONS

Cover design by Doowah Design.
Cover image: "Dance the Night Away," photo-montage by Jessie Parker.
Photo of Sue MacLeod by Oriana Leman.

This book was printed on Ancient Forest Friendly paper.
Printed and bound in Canada by Hignell Book Printing Inc.

We acknowledge the support of The Canada Council for the Arts and the Manitoba Arts Council for our publishing program.

Library and Archives Canada Cataloguing in Publication

MacLeod, Sue, author
Mood swing, with pear / Sue MacLeod.

Poems.
ISBN 978-1-927426-83-8 (paperback)

I. Title.

PS8575.L49M66 2016 C811'.54 C2016-901626-9

Signature Editions
P.O. Box 206, RPO Corydon, Winnipeg, Manitoba, R3M 3S7
www.signature-editions.com

In memory of Maude MacLeod
(1917–2010)

CONTENTS

Where the sound comes through

Gods are pushing swings in the morning light

Some of them wear bright lipstick
and laugh among themselves.
Some wear jeans as they walk among you.
One grinds a cigarette butt under her heel.
No one needs to tell you
your gods are truer than the others. You know
the great warm hands that lift you
to his shoulders. You know the scent and
pulse of his neck. You know the quaver
in her voice when she sings about the little lambs.
Wheee! she says, anticipating your pleasure,
and props you on top of the slide.
No one has told you
even the best of them won't be around
when you come to the bottom, at least
not with their big arms
open, wide.

The proportion of warm to cool

You find a whole morning in your pocket, stretch
it across your window. The wind
frantic with magpies.

— Lorri Neilsen Glenn

An unmarried woman considers Colville and his wife

(after two Alex Colville paintings side by side at the Art Gallery of Ontario)

Thirty-three years between *Woman in Bathtub* and
Woman on Ramp,
coming out of the ocean—

No one will know me
like this.

This isn't envy,
not exactly. Not with Colville
lurking, looking ominous in his robe.

Her nipples are the only warm colour.

She is

> *Woman doing Headstand*
> *Woman with Revolver*
> woman taking bath…

The water demarcates her
legs like ankle socks,
recalls a time before even he

had seen her.
Her pubic hair rises above shoreline:
well-treed island

and her hand, submerged—
a submarine, a shark, a separate consciousness.

She is now
an old woman, in bathing suit,
holding both rails.
He paints

the hang of loose flesh
on her arm. He paints how low
her breasts have fallen.

Is she thinking, *look away for once*
or is she stopped
as I am

by the heat
seeping in to later Colvilles
and because he's got it right again:

the delicate detailing
of collarbone,
how this is not diminished.

A shadow falls to one side like a cape
and she's reaching

out of it.
And—this is envy, exactly—
she's still a swimmer. He is still her witness.

Who else could see her in this light?

How will I find you?

(after Susan Low-Beer's About Face *sculpture exhibition at David Kaye Gallery on Queen Street West, Toronto)*

How will I know you
        from so many
in a white space
on a long street
where people from the mental hospital come this
                                                                        close—

Look for the broken one   the Housemaid says
He is born of spilt milk and the fallen cup
I have swept up the pieces, rough bits, shiny,
puzzled them together

What have they wound around the wound?
What have they wound around the wound?
the Prince of Homonyms
keeps asking
on a street where people come this
                                    close—

where are you from?

I see your lips sealed tight against the blizzard
see the pure hard landscape
that you bring
its twigs of rust and bits of colour
stunted glorious vegetation
You approach me and the wall
behind you, white,
starts to particulate

We travel far to find each other,
come this close to
grace
Look at everyone you meet &
See her well &
See him well

insists the Prince of Riddle.
What is:

not mass-produced
but has been fired
in the same mold?

How to make love

(i)

the proportion of warm to cool, dark to light,
these applications can continue endlessly:

a sympathy learned
of the materials & means

liberties to be taken
become evident

the hands are performing
to their own accord

vitrify (become glasslike)

the fire will now add its comment

(ii)

shapes can be cupped
mouth-to-mouth

in the deepest of relief.

In answer to your questions about love

Whatever does she see in him?

(i)

The power of attraction
(& it is boundless)

wind-driven clouds bellying like a sail

(ii)

The suave lines of willow branches!

(iii)

Reach down to its face:

who shall dare to say
that a potato is
inferior
to a pomegranate?

(iv)

Any single object by its isolation:
a little bush on a bare hill

here, we have the reason
for the lack of sharpness

(v)

We have all, spellbound

(vi)

Her very soul, if one may use the expression:
the effect of real light on an impossible tree

Can this *be love?*

There is no need for an essay

Every detail was the best of its kind—

the pond, old sheds, & the very ducks themselves.

Mood swing, with pear

The pear that wasn't eaten—
gone soft in the bowl.
I take it away and grief
surprises me. A gift so lovely
not accepted. The skin a mild yellow,
stem curved and woody, still
bearing the weight.
                                        I admire
how the upper slopes
spread out to the larger
bottom—
                              quintessential
pear—
                    and I think
                    about snowmen, when they melt, head first,
on bright, mild days,
                    lopsided
like long green pears
or self-possessed like this one:
                                                  a messenger
not from the tropics but smelling of meadows, of summer
a few orchards over,
a softly freckled boy
from across the fields.

This pear I didn't eat—now I look
closely—has tiny black dots
like a
                                                  five o'clock shadow

                                        on a man I may have
waltzed with in a bar or
on a kitchen floor
like this one, which I waltzed across
on my own just now when I was innocent

of the first pale bruises forming
in the fruit bowl,
scooting along in my purple socks
at bedtime, anticipating
coffee in the grainy
morning light.

After reading "Michiko Dead"

> *He manages like somebody carrying a box*
> *that is too heavy, first with his arms*
> *underneath.*
> —Jack Gilbert

I'm carrying not a box, but a big clay pot.
Not a death.
Thanks God, my Persian friend—
I haven't seen him
in a while—might say. But a sadness for something less
lovely than I'd hoped. A gigantic
clay pot. And I've done this before.
With groceries. A long-ago
marriage. Halfway home you know it was a big
miscalculation but there's no
turning back.
                    I start with the pot on its side,
right arm in the hollow, left arm stretched
around the girth.
When this starts to hurt I turn it upright,
Full Frontal Embrace. Once, I saw
an ad for a djambi drum:
new skin, mellow sound. Nothing to do but
keep moving. The fear
is that something will give. The sun turns
hot, I want
to roll my sleeves up. I slide
the pot lower, fingers cliff-hanging
the rim. Arch my back. Stick one hip out
for balance. Think
of Jack Gilbert with
his box of grief.
                    Who might I be, at this point,
if I hadn't read those books, lived in this
place, rounded a corner and met
but never really knew

a man from a distant country?
        This as I struggle home
from the plant shop. An unseasonable
May morning. Hands sweaty and
sweatier. Buds still forming
fists. I sway further back
as if
        to do the limbo, trick
        the pot
into thinking
it's resting against me, while
a drop of perspiration starts
its solitary trek along
my nose.

You could fall down on your knees
to progress. Anybody's progress. All
our available muscles in use.
                Yet, if I carried
this pot every day, my spine might curve, hip misalign.
And that would be deformity, not growth.
A distinction worth noting
despite the advantage of building—
and anyway, who asked for them? it wasn't me
who asked for them—stronger arms.

Counting down (an invitation?)

10 reasons for september

because of sharp pencils, unsullied erasers

because of opening, first opening, the hinged
lid of a box of 48 or even 60—

nights, with the first undercutting of *crisp*

serious wooden rulers with a strip (or is it core?) of metal

because we need something to measure by, like your watch, your
impossibly sleek & expensive—
you have laid it on the table

who's to say how long have we
been talking

because of school supplies, I was speaking of school supplies: the
translucent gold liquid, the nipple-like tip on the glue

because I once knew a Woman Who Had Seven Children
and cried at the window
first time the schoolbus went up the lane & there was no one
of hers

because of twilight:
birdsong at your window, glass
of Jameson on the side, angular line of your
wrist, light burnishing the fine
dark hairs, that time when
everything is oiled, about
to turn

because I met you in September, it was chilly when we walked along
the waterfront, you took your jacket off & slipped it
around my shoulders

shoulder season

like September, when I met you, a time when it might be feasible
to fly

my pillow, the slope of

my pillow, which isn't the slope of

send me "the pillow that you dream on"

I mean to tell you, I've always been dancing with my head on someone's
shoulder to an old
country song

Do Not Drive on the Soft—

your left shoulder coming to meet
        (we are as paper
                        dolls)

my right

shoulder: to take it. Bear
the weight

8 things you must never let anyone take from you

memory of wind, riffling through branches

don't let the bus take
(what is yours?)

the last bite of anything
(*we want to live! we want to live!*
we want to live! until our lives
are through)

the children are as sharp, as self-contained as
well, you can imagine. The bus a bright Crayola box
heading up the lane

memory of wind, first leaves carried to the forest floor

first time you feel yourself winded, wearing
down

weight of my fingertips, balanced on yours

the inevitable
crackling beneath your boots, the leaves
turned brown turned golden

I took a turn

I turned around & the floor was gone
          from underneath me

yr turn

mine &—

who would *this* be? *her* turn now?

the wheels of the seasons—
round & round! & the turning

of the page

6 lines about pages

white
new fallen

these, the sticks I lay
in careful patterns
for you to follow
to my door

5 readings of all this snow

it is God's white-out, says the Student. It covers up every mistake

new on the market, says the Cosmetician, covering every mistake

& I say
it covers memory. True, you know the Commons has been green in summer,
in September when we met but do you really
know?

it's a place to leave your footprints when you come to my door,
says the Housewife

come in from the cold, says the Lover
We will be angels soon enough. Let's go
lie down

4 reasons for gloves

a necessity for making snowballs, given all this weather

because we grew into them, from mittens, & are secretly
still proud

because gloves has the word "love" in it, also the word "solve"

so then, hand in hand

3 signs of spring

bare hands, & the deep exhalation of
breath. My breath. Yrs. The mulchy breath rising where the roots push
through

me at the window, rolling my sleeves up in the hope of cheerful April,
swishing my skirts for July

the first swell of pregnancy. That, or She wouldn't have
had all those children, not have stood wet-eyed not
watching them go

with my bare eyes

the better to watch you, my dear
I know, I've grown too narrow in my focus

I may not know the difference
between good-bye & an invitation (said
the snow
against the north wall
to the first
bloom

of forsythia)

but I know I'm speaking mainly
about school supplies, as I
told you before

1 reason for glasses

(here I go again, your glasses)

once the kissing starts, the first thing you take off

no reason?

for you to go.

The rightful

My brain is a computer that needs to be defragged.
Last week I climbed in, sorted
through the memories.
The white shirts on the line, still damp, spelled T T T:
a line of trouble stretching from the house to the wood shed.
They flapped and shivered
          steaming at my nose like fresh air
multiplied, intensified.
Grass pestered my ankles. And the roar
of surf teased my ears
with the echo
                    of an older
beat, too faint
to follow. There is just this gritty residue.

At first his taste, his scent, seemed familiar.
David. His name meant Beloved.
I married him and brought him to this shore.
I've spurned anything romantic since.
You can take your bed of roses and your
hyphenated monograms.
You can lead a man to water if you mix him with a good stiff drink.

Defrag—what kind of language am I speaking?
The wild horses of desire are on the loose again.
Far from here, the prairie spreads its golden limbs and is waiting
shamelessly for the stampede.
                    I wring my hands, I wring my arms my legs, I run, still
dripping.

Sookie sookie Sue. He quoted Steppenwolf. The band, I mean.
My real true love will circumnavigate the island.
Thunderous lyrics.
          Waves, beyond our power to unfold.

Parliamo presto, I have to hang up.
The moon is pouring silver buckets on the water now. The shirts
are iridescent on the line and a man I am about to meet is on his way
to claim them.

The aunts & the uncles, they wouldn't sit still for their pictures but I caught them anyway

banished to the front step where my mother
sent me

Edna (there's some kind of smudge on this photo)

No, that's just smoke where a face oughtta be.
Edna driving up the lane the gravel spewing,
the flat of one leathery hand of one gardener's hand on the
wheel & the radio going. It
looked like her cigarette-was-glued-to-her-lip-the-way-it-
wagged-when Edna spoke.
Thumbs green fingers yellowed

Sadie turned the other (pink) cheek

Sadie with her sleek brown hair, walking home
from The Point, home to her mother's
home she returned to
from two years in Boston, one year in Hartford,
boyfriend
she lost
in the war.
Sadie's taken off her apron &
her white cap with its tartan swatch
but you can see white caps. And the profile of Smokey
across the water. Sadie stooped a little
frown line in her forehead
shadow of something
not in the frame

Helen, with strawberry blonde hair, & nobody knew

where it came from. She hummed country music & left lipstick on the rims
of cups. Helen, the baby. But here she is waving & her fingers
have grown long & slim like all of her. The wind's waving too
in this picture & tossing her
strawberry hair. See the signaling of branches in the alder?
Helen's hem flipped back, tanned knee exposed

The uncles staggered one by one

hoorah! hoorah! & was it never   funny. I took my Polaroid hurried away
from those big swaying men, dust clouds forming underneath their boots
the
          flowers
trampled.
          I whipped round the house having caught one quick shot
                                                                                                    of a fender

just before it brought
          the clothesline down. & a shadow   falling. They smelled of
beer or of something about to go bad but there are no smells in my
photographs.

I leaned away from the wind, pulled out pictures formed already.
Like I vaguely pictured I was
formed already, in my mother's body.
And here's what she saved me from
when she chose my father: from how the uncles staggered, one by one
on bad days.

Through the swinging door

(i)

Sadie died this spring.
This house is full
of cancer. You taste it
in the metal tang
of every
fork & spoon. And on these dishes
with their roses eaten
practically away. All day you try to not
touch things
too closely, or breathe
the same air Sadie
breathed. Still,
you keep expecting her
to walk in
in her waitress outfit, ease
her shoes off, sit down
with your mother. I wish
I had your pep, she'd always tell you.
Sadie had time for
one more cigarette, another
cup of tea

(ii)

She came all the way
from Connecticut, all the way
from the dining room
into the kitchen.
Where's my Sadie?
Isn't Sadie at my table? smiling.
And the breadknives halted
in mid-slice.

Dishes stopped
rattling on their trays.
You imagine, in the moment
before Helen
started sobbing,
there was just the spell of held
breath in the kitchen,
the door whickering
back into place.

Sestina, with scrub-brush & moon

The old moon bumps against the child's window,
a helium balloon caught under the eaves, spilling
light on the table, the letter she's sending a friend. She's dotted all the i's with circles,
written Canada, the World,
the Universe in careful hand. She wakens, startled, in her bed
tucked under the window, as the moon makes its escape.

The flannelette sheets are warm, like the place before knowledge, but she can't escape
the chill the moon leaves as it spins from her window
leaving her, white-boned, alone in her bed.
She pulls the curtain back to black night. On the bay, a patch of moonlight spills.
She hears the *wish-wishing* of her mother's scrub-brush moving through the world,
the house, in circles

while the moon rolls over, throws light through the window of the city aunt, who circles
each summer, back to this village she'll never escape.
Is she thinking of a ballroom lit with worldly
chandeliers and laughter, as she sashays past her window?
Strong thumbs flick the catches open. Red and yellow silks come spilling
out of her battered suitcase, onto her childhood bed.

In the room next door, another aunt slips into bed,
white uniform with tartan apron folded over chairback. Circles
under eyes. She holds her tongue so the word that looms there can't spill
out. Then there would be no escape.
She used to be the pink-cheeked aunt, waving at the window.
Now she sinks against the pillow, breathes into the world

while downstairs, the bachelor uncle is watching world
news with the sound off, each night before bed.
They say he isn't right. You could watch him through the window,
sing to himself—*diddle dee dee*—and scratch his head; his fingers move in circles.
All day long the whistling kettle lets the steam escape.
When the tea grows strong he drinks with both feet tapping. Nothing spills

except for the silver-grey hair of the grandmother, spilled
across her pillow—coarse, like rope to hold the boats at dock. To what world
will she go, in sleep's escape?
From bed,
the child listens to the *wish*-brush, circling.
Her mother will not stop, she thinks, will not gaze through the window

at the moon—impossible like Santa Claus—spilling light through children's windows
all around the world. *Hey diddle diddle,* sings the one who isn't right. The brush
moves in circles, the child lies in bed, not knowing what she will inherit. Or escape.

I have written for beginners

or for those who have forgotten all they knew

Take 1 sight, & you will be bewildered
Take 2, & light dawns

Forget
how the earth spins round
the sun

motionless stars

inconceivable

distances away

For the moment accept—pretend—that you do know:

You are in Italy at 1100 hours local time
You are somewhere in Canada
You are in the North Sea

It is a long time
since the Sun crossed the Greenwich meridian

~

It is hardly ever as bad as this

You will see the Sun

swing

attached to a pendulum

Funnels of distant ships

reach into the sky

~

If a line were drawn from the center of the Earth
through you & out into
space, it would lead to
your zenith

for example, on a winter's morning

arrows pointing

where a single figure is found.

12 snakes & 8 ladders

Apolitical poems are also political,
and above us shines a moon
no longer purely lunar.

— Wisława Szymborska

It is time to turn on the moon.
It is time to live by a different light.

— Nancy Willard

At my next incarnation

At my next incarnation, when asked
what creature I want to be
I'll choose the hummingbird
for good looks
and the taste
of nectar

or the eagle.
There I'll find a faithful husband,
learn the hard blood craft
of a predator, dance
cartwheels in the sky.

At my next incarnation
I am tumbling through the grass
blades and come upon
the Small House in the Clearing.

A bouquet of Indian corn
nailed to a wooden door.
Through the glass:
shelves of books,
a guitar with a long black neck and gleaming
belly, a stove
for the arts of fire.

Who makes all this?
I want to be a maker, too.
I'll be one of these.

The surrounding trees are invaded then
by a wingless flock,
each one proclaiming louder
than the next,
the incessant
cry of the personbird:
it's *me*!   it's *me*!

The tribe who worshipped children

They're building a new civilization at the seaside.

So a wandering anthropologist might say
should he come here from some further shore,
his back to the main lodge
with waiters on the patio, facing
what I'm facing now:
log cabins on the beach.

The people here could not escape
the sanctity of sea and sky.

My daughter and some friends she's made
come striding through the waves.
He'd see no sign of want. No strife. No unjust
distribution. He'd see us
as her social studies book
saw
the Coast Salish:

The land was rich in fruits and berries
and the sea was full of fish.

Imagine how he'd hunt for mores, rituals.
He'd find her jeans and t-shirt
on the doorstep where she dried them, flat
like paper dolls,
held down where the tabs would go
by stones, big as fists.
Would he take this for some life-sized game?
Or make of it an altar?
Would we become

the tribe who worshipped children?

Light glancing off the water is so bright
he'd have to shield his eyes
the way I'm shielding mine—there's just
this huge horizon
where children wade in from the sea,
children who are ours.
They haven't pulled out plump and smiling
salmon for our supper; they've
built a castle—grainy, tall—and
kicked it down
with small, hard feet and

hours of daylight left, to build again.

Glimpse

He's always been a shy boy.
So what she notices first—looking up
from her place in line and glimpsing
him, like a stranger—is the confident
swing to his limbs.
One hand grazes
the metal rail as he pauses
with the others, shoulders broad and sloping
like his dad's.
Ape, the kids in the lane used to chant.
God save us
from a baseball glove that barely
got used, from the furious
blinking-back. Now he's come into his own;
he'd laugh, but into his
masculine grace is how she
thinks of it. Big arms resting
at his sides, at ease.
The hesitant bent to his head is
there, like always.
But as she watches, his face lifts and breaks
into a smile—a nod to the boy beside him.
Young man, she means.
All these mother's children
moving all at once
from her line of vision.
Not because it's her turn
to step up to the teller's cage.
It *is*. But she needs to show somebody, anyone,
the woman behind her:
my son, up there,
pointing to the tv
suspended on its axis.
But the camera has already moved on, is sweeping
through streets of Kabul.

It will swing back a few minutes later
for a final
domestic perspective: a shot
of more troops on their way.

If I had my way with death

When my time comes I'd like to disintegrate instead, please.
The word "corpse" holds no appeal,
and I've always been embarrassed
by the burps and rumblings,
a bit disappointed
we didn't get something more elegant, discreet—
a design more in keeping with the ethereal
nature of spirit, of mind.
Though I'm grateful for these eyes and hands,
these arms that recall the firmly packed weight
of an infant in terrycloth sleepers
—the scent of her: take *milk*, take *dew*—
and a husband, his chest, my ear pressed to his heartbeat
in the middle of the dance. And what comes to mind first:
the particulars

of this very afternoon:
tickle of grass at my nose
and the forget-me-nots, gone gangly, doing backflips
as I mowed them down,
and how rhubarb floating in a sink
can sound like rolling
logs, or—if you close your eyes longer, feel only
the sluicing of cool
water at your wrists—a slow-building drum roll
in the neighbouring village.
Black river in between.
What a gift to just go on like this, sniffing babies
and slicing rhubarb stalks and sailing
downriver on a barge
like Miss Rumphius, to be serenaded
by the local chief, and holding the wine glass
by its bowl, and now its stem,
laughing with these friends across the table
and reading books, reading books

until one day—gone
like the words on the last—

            No "courageous battles lost" in the obituaries
if I had my way.
                    Just relief when anyone
late for anything, shows up.
And reports of final sightings:
Last seen by the caddie, seventeenth hole.
Last seen en route to the library.
Last seen by his parents, tucking him in.
      He was laughing to himself, they'd say. And say again.
      The bright yellow birds on the mobile were making their rounds.
Last seen jaywalking
into a gap between cars

like my father did last week
(eighty-five, but still needed right here,
thanks). Little blue-eyed guy? big nose, big hands,
who beams up at the CN Tower
from his ninth-floor window
and crosses the street to the greenhouse and benches at Allan Gardens.

He crossed ahead of me
and for a minute I couldn't see him anywhere.
Could this be it?
In all this bustle he adores.
Saving himself, and both of us, from untold
pain and trouble. Hand raised,
as confident as Moses.
Gone in a puff, of exhaust.

Circa 1930

My father dreamt he was a boy again
in Sydney.

There was a water trough:
a circle
where three streets met
and the horses
were taking long drinks.

There'll be no one left
with memories to quench a thirst like this one.

Said my father, I could nearly
reach out and touch them.

Poem beginning with a line by Jack Gilbert

Mildness more and more the danger.
And I heed your words. Hope
I'm not imagining this life
to be less mild

than it looks.
A day like this, I'm grateful for
my thick socks on the wide-board floors,
the heat kicking in and a long
backyard view.
                    Old dog asleep
on the rug beneath my desk.
I step into the kitchen.
Blinds up.
Just past suppertime in February.
Snow.

I watch it
cap
the fenceposts,
settle in the crooks
of many-elbowed trees. How
do they not mind the cold? And
if this wasn't enough—

          reflected
  through the study window

          beaming
  from a nest of branches, my

          computer screen

shimmering. Blue.

My furnace runs on oil; let's not kid ourselves.
We're devouring every second.
I'm ambivalent about computers, Jack.
Yet—how it floated:

Pastoral, with iMac.

Snow still falling.
Mildness. Or the opposite?
A contentment deep as that.

Poem beginning with a line from bedbugger.com

And then the bugs took to the ceiling,
writes the girl in Brooklyn.
They had a stepladder ready
They sprayed the overhead lamp—

Steri-fab, Bedlam,
powder of diatomite:
language of infestation, of desperation

—and packed
their things in Ziploc bags
big enough to hold god's
leftovers.
Her many books, his guitars.
A bed bug can live 18 months
without food, dreaming
blood and waiting
for the bag to open

can get into
your computer, drawn
to heat.

If a planet
over-heating, sucked dry by a hungry
implacable species… if a planet
had a mother, she too
would race through darkness
on the L train
with a steam cleaner, still in its box.

Worst of all, writes the girl,
being bit on the eyelids.

They wore sleep masks
They wore ear plugs
Made a path

of double-sided tape around the bed
and lay there—bait

and woke to bugs
from all directions
trapped on the strong adhesive.

I would drown them,
writes the girl, instructively—
this girl in Brooklyn who would start her days
by dousing
bed-bug-studded
strips of tape in poison,
In case they might be suffering,
stuck like that.

Vegetarian poem, with a line by Albert Schweitzer

(i)

You will no longer partake

You may be unsure
& you may wonder

sweet potato lotus root cereal (see label)
brown basmati or wehani millet amaranth

You may feel at a loss as to what to do with tofu

almond butter cashew butter pumpkin seeds (unroasted)
When bread is rising at the bakery

beans (adzuki) sprouts (alfalfa)
or on your kitchen counter

collard greens black turtle beans
science is just beginning
to understand

cruciferous vegetables allium vegetables
There are more than 11,000 kinds of legume

You may feel at a loss as to what to do

(ii)

"The man is truly ethical
Rinse sprigs of parsley with cool water

who shatters no ice crystal
Lay 3 or 4 beans side by side on the cutting board

as it sparkles in the sun
Choose a zucchini 4 to 8 inches long

tears no leaf from a tree."
It will be younger & more tender

You may feel at a loss.

Some days, we're all domesticated animals

Dog reclining on the floor.
Now that he's old
he follows me from room to room
and sinks down—sack
of elbows. What does he think
I can save him from?
Our small rotations

monitored
by the cat
on the piano top,
flexing
her claw pads and lazily
complaining.

In her guilty
throat a warbling,
like birds.

In the original, yellow-covered book

overwhelming scenes of waterfalls & rocky
cliffs

bird flaps its wings

we can just discern a hermit's hut, these
shadowy sages, looking rather small

bird flaps its wings (cont'd)

There are typically 12 snakes & 8 ladders

Rules vary. Home
must be reached on an exact throw.

Real horses are a nuisance in this setting

Omen

The instant the tips of his thumb & index finger
touch the piece in question

Knocking it over accidentally—sleeve gets caught—is
considered a bad omen

Travelogue

A bishop on a white square
no matter how fond of travelling, will never
set foot on a black square

~

By a mere small movement
she influences the entire constellation

~

What can be done with a man
who has reached the other side, & is not
allowed to turn around?

~

They are more voluminous
than their riders
The possibility of a trap
must always be borne in mind

Introduction to heroics

The creatures that became
chess pieces

in the Middle Ages, in the West,
began to change basic form

Fantasy, dynamism, temperament
In the position to be this bold

Until this point
it was the everyday work of mortals

She runs like a bishop, &
charges like a rook

The Queen had exposed herself to fire
from 3 sides

Five hard truths

Defeating a caliph was not without its dangers

Diligence is not a bad substitute for talent

The second-best move is often the only correct one

Real horses are a nuisance in this setting

Every move should affect the whole board

Two more truths, harder

At some point we realize
the game's attraction does not lie in social contact
but, generally speaking,
in opposition

The sacrifice of a queen
regarded by onlookers as the ultimate pleasure.

Household hint (floors)

Yes,

I am suggesting that you get

down

on your

knees.

Anything else is just a shortcut.

Spent

A woman sleeps late
because she can, arm curved
beneath her head. In her dream
the word "serum,"
sad ape

swinging in a bone-

dry cage,

In her dream there are so many steps downtothesubwayso
namelessmanyfaces&a
gradually clarifying blur of black &

white. tile. which. gleams.

The train bursts
from the tunnel, arcs
into space. Through the glass

sudden vista
of moon.

She brings the camera to her eye to catch
the craters, catch the pearl
grey sky

curve
of the satellite's
impenetrable skin. This
final proof
of
unlivability.

As she shoots
a smell
of sharp pine rises,

Christmas burning
on the distant planet. The firing
of old flashbulbs, spent
& milky.

World history (ii)

With the invention of a bow & arrow, a whole new family of

stringed instruments appeared

You may want to embellish:

small step
from
zing of bow

to
strum of string

back in the camp, recounting.

Information desk (Spring Garden Road library)

I pull some fresh non-fiction from the truck
and head for the display: a wall of
disappearing wildlife and exploding
oil wells, child prostitution,
robotics (*Why the Future Doesn't Need Us*),
torture, rising water marks, and all
is as usual:
Some of the regulars/irregulars
are looking for dates on the computers.
That old guy who shouldn't leave home
without a hearing aid
is pointing to titles on
the stack of index cards he carries,
with a nicotine-stinking finger,
while Lynn, leaning across the desk, bellows
good-naturedly into his ear.
Nearly time for my break.
Sun, and the smell from the Bud the Spud chip truck
pour in through the tall, old-fashioned windows.
From where I'm standing, I can't see over
the edge of this raft.
I can't even feel the motion.

Narrative painting

(after an untitled work by Jim Parsons,
Lower Prospect, Nova Scotia)

The candlestick divides her face,
obscures it from the painter
(as he sketches, across the table).
She leans forward, talks
with the other woman.
Yellow hair, mauve dress, hint
of a ruffle at her neck and yet
so adamant. The bottle of wine
at her elbow full-
bellied, brown and as
solid as earth, as the man
in the foreground, one hand a fist
on the table like a paw,
the other drawn up to his chin—
The Thinker. We are all
of this. And the room
with its tall cupboards and what might be
a scattering of dishes on the counter
is a Left Bank café with its
poets and painters, is a
Nova Scotia kitchen
where we are
two women talking
(rocky shore, gusty night)
one man sitting slightly apart
(another, sketching).
And the burst
flame of the candle
is halo, is
sun, and I haven't mentioned
the plate, cut off at the edge
of the table, hand-painted boldly

in the indigos of a warmer
sea, which makes it seem like
something calling to us, beckoning
from another hemisphere, one
we haven't found yet
in the oldest stories.

Where the sound comes through

Where the sound comes through

in memory of Diane Moore (1951-2003)

There was a grey cast to the sky
        & Diane's dark hair, billowing
        She was wearing those boots, not cowboy but similar
She had a line on some secondhand store
no one else had located

        It was bleak
        It was April
        We met on the doorstep and walked downtown
        two single mothers
        downstairs / upstairs
        poet / dancer

        a *maverick* in dance—
        it would say in her obituary eight months later

        We came to a ridge of snow, porous & charcoaled
        as if a stream of smoke from the stacks across the harbour
        had solidified &
landed at our feet. Diane
                        leapt over it
                                        First, she kicked it with the toe of

her boot & said
she *liked* late winter:

                    We've got the last laugh on all of this
                    We know what's just around the corner

Just
her boyfriend's footsteps, Peter's
footsteps on the floor above me

(bright scarf looped around his neck
as if he's taking on the feminine

Friends gone by now &
white-haired mother

& Geoff
to come home on study break, pack up his things

just Peter's
steps/steps
amplified in
empty rooms

cleaning out
her closets
finding
knocking on my door one morning
—*hey, you might be interested*—
poems
she wrote when she was twenty

There are people who irritate you, frankly
extroverts who laugh too loud
too musically too often
high-priestess cackle in the stairwell
who park in your spot without asking
who park in your spot when you've asked them not to
though they'll lend you their car
with greatest generosity, so
"American," though they aren't
who have corrected you once on the Commons
for throwing your apple core
in the garbage can not on the grass
who comment that you appear to be very new
to gardening

whose steady stream of
company starts to look like
a statement on your affinity
for solitude
who leave the lids off things
even when they go away
you know that's why there's suddenly
a mouse problem
who once lived in a house with rats and seem
to find the whole thing funny

who clomp down the stairs like a
teenager nobody's told to be quiet
give a kick a
flourish
on their way

~

the striking of the Gong!

10 years
of Sunday meetings

What begins as one small o*mmmm*

expands un*tillllll*
you'd swear
your house, invaded
by a giant
bee

the bricks old plaster walls & pine planks guzzling furnace sump pump
moaning under
neath your feet about to spread transparent
wings
& yet

i*nnnnnn*
places where the sound comes through most clearly
you can trace a single voice
like a thread through the cloth

An older couple at your door:
We come to chant?

Upstairs, you say with so*mmmme*
regret

A kidney transplant long before, when she was young—this meant years on anti-rejection drugs. Over time, some of these lead to greater risks of cancer.

Years
she might not have had.
Is this why she opens
each day like a—*no, be more precise, be more* Diane *about it*—
holds it in the palm of her hand, say, with an eyebrow raised:

Hello then. What's in here?

Nursing my coffee I glance out the window:

Diane
making me feel like a slug again.

I swing the screen door open, cat
darts out. Pull my bathrobe tighter, step out to the garden

What's up? Aside from *her,* that is, it was one of her legs
dangling through the foliage
caught my attention.
I don't even ask how she managed to climb
into that fork in the branches, pruning sheers in hand to cut a bigger
sky

❧

It takes a village
to raise a crow

A united front of aunts & uncles set
to swoop

on anyone who dares
trespass

near the spot where some adolescent, cocky-winged,
has landed on a perch & then—

when fear-of-flight sets in—
is stuck there, dumb as weathervane

For hours for days the whole block a cawing a warning of
swarming

like worms when they squirm in a bucket: How vital
this is! & you thought it was just an accessory, or
backdrop to your own eternal busy-
                ness

On Charles Street, two women stand in the din.
The upstairs woman paces:

"How long can it go without water?"
Together, they regard

the teenage bird
shuffling on the fence that surrounds the oil tank

a slightly smaller replica of those who keep watch
But O! its indecipherable
eye

The downstairs woman wants to call someone—

the upstairs woman interrupts. *We'll send the kids out—*
in their bike helmets. They can put a bowl of water on the post

Some years later when a crow is preening in a branch outside her window
the downstairs woman will phone her daughter:

Do you remember that racket the crows
would make on Charles Street?

Because she has a different view now, she imagines the scene from
a bird's perspective, or that of something

higher. A dive bomb—crows from all directions, water
bowl dashed

to the gravel.
Two twelve-year-olds are racing

for the long green house, the mothership:
Are you guys nuts?

The houses all along the back lane rocking on the wingbeats;
clotheslines   tether them

The first term of university
is not a good time to move house
or even redecorate
the room your child will come home to
at Christmas
Surely she got the same brochures
The summer before
your child starts university is not
a good time for
one side of your body to stop
following directions
Not the time to learn the meaning
of *aggressive*
when applied to brain tumour,
to comprehend
stage three
Not a good time for the drugs
that help a body accept a new kidney
after all these years to turn,
stir up their own
last laugh

Damp wall of sheets that I crest up against

drop by
drop
young woman
leaching
out
of me

a ticking

in my quiet room &

something dragging, rolling

on the floor above &

rush of steps

was it the nightsweat woke me up?

or Diane   upstairs   falling

I've read Jack Gilbert's poem
where he helps Michiko to the chamber pot
& despite his *heart as helpless as crushed birds,*
at the line, *How strange & fine*
to get so near to it, I always hate him for a second.
It was everything, that autumn:
my daughter grown, & *whoosh*—
a vacuum, but lighter, more
buoyant, & someone, when I least
expected, stepping on
to join me.
The now-familiar progress
of a cane above the ceiling:
life is *short, life* is *short.*
And Peter, bellowing up the stairs
to somebody,
I'm going to bring Diane up now.
This is before they put the chair lift in.
This is the fine print at the bottom
of the contract
they mightn't have come to for years.
And here's me:
riding into the brink of something
on a south shore road with both feet
on the dashboard of a
small black truck.
Johnny Cash, just dead, is
belting out *one foot on Jacob's ladder*
Jim & me along with him
& the sun belting down & the
first of the leaves letting
go of their branches
spiralling & turning
everything to
tunnel

~

I believe there is a fundamental difference

poets   write metaphors
dancers   act them out

Jim dropped me off that night
& I knew it

by the howling laughing singing wailing
pounding feet & whining of the chair lift
            up/down
            up/down
            up/down
            up
            loading it up
            they were
            loading it with stuff & then it
            sounded like they

            ripped it off its track

Hold this a minute, says Peter's sister
I take one end of the trunk & think my back might break
blood rushing to my fingers
Then she hoists it onto *her* back
& practically skips down the stairs

I follow with a spider plant, a box of cutlery

A performance artist, Peter's sister. Physical comedy. I've seen her.
All five feet

As the van turns the corner onto Robie Street for the last time
I think what strong women have spent time
in these rooms, nearly
impervious

~

You show the place
for the co-op
You pause

with one prospective member
at the height chart
Diane pencilled on the wall

This is way too fast—

but you'll be glad
soon

of the signs again
of other lives
in tandem

hints of spices
drifting to the entryway &
ringing phones & running
footsteps
everything but
ommmm

~

There are people
who ask you up for dinner
but don't get time to
make anything but the soup & aren't a bit
embarrassed & the soup is rich
& bountiful
who have been known to go
to meetings with their i.v. in
who have been known to be
opinionated
at meetings

who say *we sat in a room &*
smoked our brains out for the first two years
& he's a keeper
& the third summer climbed Gros Morne
people who look to the mountaintop with impunity
who say *once the kids are gone*
you should come upstairs
we'll smoke those joints we never
got around to

& finally
who smile
with a wool cap like a tea cosy over their baldness
& say things like *hey, have you seen*
my new 'monorail'?
& do you want a demo?
people
who'll get on & push a button
& give a wave like in a parade
as they're ascending
people who set a standard
you now have to meet for the rest of your life
this gift they left you
that you never
asked for.

Notes and acknowledgements

Poems in this book have appeared, sometimes in different versions, in the following journals and magazines: *The Antigonish Review*, *Event*, *Grain*, *Our Times* and *Room of One's Own*; the following anthologies: *The Art of Poetic Inquiry* (Backalong Books, 2012), *Desperately Seeking Susans* (Oolichan Books, 2012), *To Find Us: Words and Images of Halifax* (Halifax Regional Municipality, 2004); and the following chapbook anthology: *About Face* (Field Notes, 2013). My thanks go out to the editors and publishers.

"An unmarried woman considers Colville and his wife" is for Kelley Aitken, with thanks for inviting me to take part in the Ekphrasis Eleven reading at the Art Gallery of Ontario in September 2010.

"Poem beginning with a line from bedbugger.com" is for Elaine Whittaker, who invited me to write about beauty and terror at the opening of her art installation, "(in)trepid cultures," at The Red Head Gallery in October 2011.

The poem "The Rightful" began as a writing exercise: Jim Simmerman's "Twenty Little Poetry Projects," in *The Practice of Poetry: Writing Exercises from Poets Who Teach*, edited by Robin Behn and Chase Twichell (HarperCollins, 1992, 2001).

I gratefully acknowledge the Toronto Arts Council for a grant that helped me complete this book. And I give warmest thanks to Karen Haughian and Clarise Foster at Signature Editions.

I'm also deeply grateful to the poetry groups I've been part of in Halifax and Toronto, with a special thanks to Marilynn Rudi for her suggestion on the Colville poem. Huge thanks, too, to Maureen Hynes for her careful reading of the whole manuscript. I'm grateful to Julie Vandervoort for early comments on "Where the sound comes through," and to Dilys Leman, along with others in Jay MillAR's long poem workshop, for critiquing this poem at a much later stage. Finally, special thanks to Deirdre Dwyer for her 11th-hour feedback.

The nine poems listed below are "compiled poems." The arrangement, line breaks and punctuation are my own, as are the titles *except* for those marked with an asterisk. But the words, phrases and sentence fragments that comprise the poems come from the how-to books and encyclopedias shown below. Note that the content is decontextualized, having no necessary relationship to its original meaning, order, or page or chapter placement. Any group of words that are unbroken by a line break or full-stop punctuation mark, *or* by capitalization to indicate a new sentence, appeared unbroken in the source text.

"How to Make Love" — *Discovering Pottery*, by Larry Memmott (Paul Hamlyn Pottery Ltd., 1989)

"In answer to your questions about love" — *The Artistic Anatomy of Trees: Their structure and treatment in painting*, by Rex Vicat Cole (Seeley, Service and Company, 1915; Dover Publications, 1965)

"I have written for beginners"* — *Celestial Navigation for Yachtsmen*, by Mary Blewitt (McGraw-Hill, 1995)

"Vegetarian poem, with a line by Albert Schweitzer" — *Becoming Vegetarian*, by Vesanto Melina (Macmillan Canada, 1994)

"In the original, yellow-covered book"* — *T'ai Chi Chih!*, by Justin Stone (Sateri Resources, 1984)

"There are typically 12 snakes & 8 ladders"* — *Oxford History of Board Games* (Oxford University Press, 1999)

"Real horses are a nuisance in this setting"* — *Encyclopedia of Chess Games* (Oxford University Press, 1981)

"Household Hint, Floors" — *The Queen of Clean: A Queen for All Seasons*, by Linda Cobb (Simon & Schuster, 2001)

"World History (ii)" — *Making Gourd Musical Instruments*, by Ginger Summit (Sterling, 1999).

About the author

Sue MacLeod has lived in Toronto; in Halifax, where she was the city's inaugural poet laureate; and now in Montréal. But her roots are firmly in Cape Breton.

Sue's poems have appeared in numerous journals and anthologies, including *The Malahat Review, Grain, Event, Room of One's Own, Coastlines: The Poetry of Atlantic Canada, The Art of Poetic Inquiry* and *Desperately Seeking Susans*. She is a past recipient of *Arc*'s Poem of the Year Award and has taught poetry at Dalhousie University and the Art Gallery of Ontario.

Sue is also a freelance editor and a fiction writer. Her first YA novel, *Namesake,* was published in 2013 to critical acclaim. *Mood Swing, with Pear* is her third book of poems.

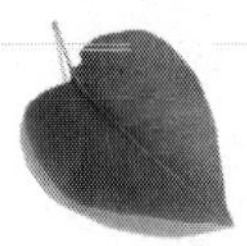

Eco-Audit
Printing this book using Rolland Enviro100 Book instead of virgin fibres paper saved the following resources:

Trees	Solid Waste	Water	Air Emissions
2	68 kg	5,587L	225 kg